HEALTHFUL HEART
B O O K S

A catalogue record for this book is
available from the British Library

FOREWORD

My dream to write a cook book has been with me since my early 20's fuelled by my Dad's nightly phone calls: "What can I put with this?" "How do I cook that?" "Why does this taste horrible?"

The initial title I had back then was 'Cooking for Dads and Divorcees' but when friends were also asking for tips, or just asking me to cook, the title became 'For girls who can't or won't cook'. As time went by I realised I just needed to just put the idea to paper to whatever title and so when my friend, Georgia, said "that'll only take you a day" I started!

That was about a year ago.

My ideas for the book have changed over time as has my attitude to food and the recognition of its importance to our health.

As a GP I am conscious of the daily impact our food choices have on our health and well-being. Our medical school training in nutrition is very sketchy. My continual research has changed my attitude to food from it requiring to light up all the pleasure centres in my brain to a diet that provides nutrients for good health, longevity and disease prevention. I aim to eat food that provides balanced nutrition and reduces health risks but I understand this is a journey which I'm loving.

This book is an introduction to plant based eating, helping the transition from an omnivorous diet including processed foods to incorporating meals which provide benefits as well as calories with the aim of becoming fully plant based. There are 'Dirty Vegan' recipes in this book, so called because they contain sugar or unhealthy fats highlighting this book as a transition to a whole food plant based diet. The book encourages meal planning, home preparation and cooking of plant based meals to enjoy. Incorporating nutritionally dense foods can literally save our lives by reversing and preventing illness.

When doctors used to smoke in the clinic room between seeing patients during my training, nobody thought cigarettes would be outlawed the way they are in modern society, so it will be around supporting our health with a plant based diet; you'll be sneaking outside for a sausage!

My inspirations and aspirations have morphed into my first cook-book: a book of recipes that are easy to follow, quick to prepare, delicious to eat and most importantly, cruelty free.

I hope you enjoy them!
Dr Hayley Tait

NOTES

In all the recipes I have specified the tools required. I've tried to keep it simple and inexpensive hoping you already have all the kit needed to get going.

I bought a stick blender from a supermarket for £7 a few years ago and it's great for blending soups. I have a small blender for hummus, pesto and herbs but I have also made many of these recipes whilst camping only using a knife, board, pan and camping stove.

Please feel free to change the recipes if you don't like any of the ingredients or if the ingredients don't happen to be in your fridge. For example, if you don't like mushrooms, just substitute with another veg, tofu or tempeh. Remember frozen veggies are great and it means you can whip up tasty, healthy food anytime.

I choose organic produce wherever possible because I think organic vegetables and fruit taste better than non-organic as well as reduce our intake of added pesticides. The more we all buy organic, the likelihood prices will reduce making them more accessible for everyone.

THANKS

To Georgia for telling me to get on with it. To Kerrie for the playful title. To Jess for starting my vegan journey with a "dairy-is-scary" clip. To Shireen of Plant Based Health Professionals who produces evidence every week to support a whole-food plant based diet for health. To all the doctors and health professionals continuing their medical education, exploring nutrition and wellness - may we become the majority and lead the way to health with disease prevention and disease reversal.

Also thanks to all the social media supporters who have liked and shared my posts from @health_on_ the_hob on Instagram and shared my journey since August 2019. Huge thanks to Joe and Jack from @uncorkedproductions who produced the photographs to showcase my food in a relaxed yet professional way. To my brother, Jay and dad, Ted who are missed every day and who I wish had been able to start this journey with me that it might have made a difference. Finally to my beautiful daughter, Hannah, my greatest critic and supporter who is unfailing in her kindness and love. She is inspirational for things that could be.

> **"Eating a plant based diet supports justice and equality for all,**
> **there is no salad too big, no artery too small."**
> **Hayley Tait, peace-loving vegan**

> **"Live as if you were to die tomorrow. Learn as if you were to live forever."**
> **Mahatma Gandhi**

Contents

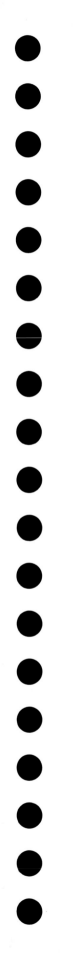

TOOLS AND TIPS

TOOLS

Knives: This is very much a personal choice but my recommendation would be to sharpen whatever you have, ironically it seems safer.

Boards: I have a variety of plastic and wood.

Pots and pans: My pans are 15 years old, predominantly stainless steel and some still have their glass lids.

Stick blender: I love this for blending soups, it makes them foamily creamy without the cream. Mine has an attachment for blending small portions of about 400mls which I mainly use for making hummus or curry pastes.

Box grater: It has all sides for zesting/finer shredding/ normal (grated carrot for coleslaw etc) and wide which I only use for the odd shapes in my Thai papaya salad. I have a mandolin that I cannot use without shredding a bit of my hand ... so I don't.

Sieve: Love a good sieve or colander! I have 4 (not yet classed as clutter) my favourite is an oldie from my niece and nephew shaped like a bowler hat and it always make me smile.

Peeler: I tend not to peel or even wash vegetables but sometimes use this if I peel cooking apples or for salads (cucumber or carrot slices coil nicely into thin curls).

Cake tins, cooling rack & baking trays: mine are ancient and are multipurpose. I like the springform cake tins but sometimes forget to resist the temptation to remove fragile sponges too soon.

TIPS

Charring

In a few recipes I mention charring the vegetables first, which involves blackening and blistering them over a flame or on the rungs of a very hot oven. 'Health on the hob on the hop' or 'On the hob in haste' it is not! But we spend a lot of time rushing round and we deserve the extra depth of flavour this method imparts on the meal.

I prefer to do this over a gas flame and take time turning the veg (commonly peppers or aubergine) as it blackens. It takes a few minutes, maybe up to 10 depending on the amount you have to do but it's worth it for the flavour. If you don't have a gas flame, put the oven up really high around 200-220 C and pop the veg directly on the rack with a tray on the rack below. Keep turning every 5 minutes and it will take about 20 minutes until the veg blackens and softens. It's important to keep the hot juices that come out when you cut it open to add to the dish but be careful you don't get scalded, particularly with peppers; or char them a few hours beforehand and rest in a tray.

Zesting

As well as the juice the zest or skin of citrus fruits gives lots of citrusy flavour to dishes. You want a fine rind and I find the best way is to use a fine grater or the fine side of a box grater rotating the fruit regularly so you get the bright, oily zest rather than the white pith. (If the fruit is waxed wash it in warm water first to remove.) Watch your fingers as you rotate quickly across the blades. Once zested, I like to roll the fruit firmly on the board to loosen the juice before cutting and squeezing the juice out.

Steam 'Frying'

Moving towards a healthful diet based around whole foods, plants and avoiding processed foods, sugar and added oils, it's a good idea to try cooking without oils. This method is remarkable, I'm surprised at how little difference it makes omitting this additional fat in the preparation.

So instead of adding a tablespoon of fat/ oil to the pan before your other ingredients, add 2-3 tablespoons of water. Once it simmers, add the prepped ingredients and don't let them go dry. Adding a lid continues the 'steam-fry' process and doesn't impact on flavour.

Soaking Beans

My good friend Susie-Q gave me this tip and it's changed my dread of soaking and cooking beans as they are delicious prepared this way. She adds an inch/ 3cm piece of dried seaweed called Kombu to the soaking water, washes it with the beans and cooks it with the beans. It not only adds subtle flavour and iodine to the broth but softens the beans beautifully. I don't have the science behind this, it just works!

Kombu is sold in Liverpool's vegan, wholefood and international shops; it's not cheap (at the time of writing this expect to pay around £6) but the packet will last ages (unless you soak industrial amounts of beans) and it doesn't go off. You can also use it to add to soups for its delicious flavour.

Chopping Herbs

As always, sharpen your knife, lay your herbs on the board. Start with the point of your knife in the top middle of the board and slice down. Keeping the point top, mid centre, fan the knife blade to the right and left of the board with your top hand above the knife, sea-sawing with the other hand chopping as you go.

Notes

Reference to oil or butter will always be plant based meaning no dairy-based spreads or butters but coconut, sunflower, olive and others. There are new brands released all the time and they are readily available in shops.

I recommend reading the whole recipe first before starting anything.

I really like using measuring cups rather than weighing and apart from in baking, most measurements can be rough.

When I use curry powder I choose a ready made spice blend from Mattas, an international supermarket on Bold Street, Liverpool, at it's amazing.

Gluten Free:

The gluten free recipes are marked with this symbol.

STARTERS, SNACKS & SIDES

GLUTEN FREE

"TEAR 'N' SHARE"
ROASTED SPICED CAULIFLOWER

Serves 4-6 as a side or starter depending on the size of cauliflower

Tools: knife/ board/ baking tray

Timings: Prep 5, cooking 40, total 45 minutes

Set the oven to 170-180 C

INGREDIENTS:

- 1 Cauliflower
- 4 teaspoons Garam masala
- Salt
- 4 Tablespoons Oil

METHOD:

1. Chop any old yellow leaves off the base of the cauliflower and score the base by making a deep cross through the tough stalk with your knife.

2. Sprinkle with 4 teaspoons garam masala, a little salt and 4 tablespoons of oil. Rub in well.

3. Bake in the oven for 30-40 minutes. Check on it mid-way and cover with foil if the top is burning. Once cooked it can rest in the foil, then you can divide it up or let everyone just take a portion. It's like a healthy tear and share.

SWEET POTATO CHIPS

The choice of paprika is yours: peppery or smokey and sweet, they both work well.

Set the oven at 180C

Tools: knife/ board/ baking tray

Timings: Prep 10, cooking 30, total 40 minutes

INGREDIENTS:

- 1 medium sweet potato per person
- Coconut or olive oil (optional)
- Half a teaspoon Paprika per potato.
- Salt and ground black pepper.

METHOD:

1. Chop the sweet potatoes into chips.

2. Toss them in 2 tablespoons of oil if using, and a teaspoon of paprika. Salt and pepper

3. Roast for 30 minutes, tossing them and shaking the tray half way through cooking.

I like the roasted cauliflower, sweet potato chips with mushy peas or some steamed broccoli.

VEGETABLE SPRING ROLLS

Makes 12 large rolls or 12-20 portions of delicious crunchiness. We love serving them with sriracha spicey sauce. Other options are sweet chilli, satay, tamarind chutney or soy.

Tools: Knife, board, pan and wok or other frying pan, box grater.

Timings: Prep 15, cooking 15, total 30 minutes

INGREDIENTS:

- 1 sheet of rice noodles cooked as per packet (usually boil for 5 minutes)
- ¼ white cabbage
- 2 carrots
- 1 stick celery
- 200g beansprouts
- 1 pack of frozen filo pastry, take out the freezer 30mins before you need it.
- 4 cloves garlic, finely chopped
- 1 inch fresh ginger, peeled and grated
- 2 birds eye chillies, finely chopped
- 6 spring onions
- 1 teaspoon turmeric powder or 2 inches of fresh finely grated
- Salt or soy sauce and pepper
- 1 litre vegetable oil for deep frying

METHOD:

1. Boil the rice noodles in hot water for 5 minutes, drain and rinse in cold water. Grate the carrot, cabbage, celery, fresh ginger and fresh turmeric if using. Chop the spring onions into thin slices and add to a bowl with the other vegetables and season with soy, pepper, garlic and chilli. Cut the noodles with scissors and add to the mix and taste to check the balance of flavour.

2. Unwrap the filo carefully so you can take one sheet at a time without exposing the rest as it dries quickly and if it's dry it won't roll. Have a small bowl of water handy.

3. Make a spring roll by placing a heaped tablespoon of mixture onto a filo square, roll once, fold in the edges and continue to roll. Dip the end edge in water and seal in a roll shape. As you make a pile keep them covered with a tea towel that is slightly damp.

4. Heat the oil in a wok or wide saucepan. It should be about 3-5cm depth. Use a sizzle test of a small piece of bread which should brown easily over 10 seconds. Be careful it's not too hot or the outsides will burn before the filling is heated. Fry the spring rolls in batches. They take about 5 minutes with regular turning to be an even deep brown colour. You can keep them warm in a hot oven while you cook the rest then serve immediately from a large plate with some sriracha sauce, tamarind chutney or chilli sauce.

HIL'S PAKORAS

When I pitched up to a new year's party prequel in London, my old school friend, Hil, was making these delicious pakora. Well, she was making something spiced and fried that was brilliant party food for later. I made up this version of events.

Tools: board/ knife/ 2 pans

Timings: Prep 10, cooking 30, total 40 minutes

INGREDIENTS:

- 2 potatoes
- 4 small or 2 large onions (I prefer to use red ones)
- 4 tablespoons chick pea (gram) flour
- 1 teaspoon curry powder
- 1 teaspoon baking powder
- 1 green chilli
- Salt and pepper
- 200ml Beer or fizzy water
- ½ cup frozen peas

METHOD:

1. Peel and chop 2 potatoes into 1cm cubes and put on to boil.

2. Peel and half 4 small onions or 2 big ones. You want to slice them really thinly in half moon shapes so that you can then split them into strands.

3. Prepare the batter with 4 tablespoons of chick pea flour (gram flour), one teaspoon curry powder, the chopped chilli to your taste, salt and pepper. Add a heaped teaspoon of bicarbonate of soda or baking powder and make it up to a thick coating batter with beer or fizzy water. It makes a fun, frothy batter.

4. After 15 minutes add 2 handfuls of peas to the boiling potatoes and cook for 3 minutes then drain and cool.

5. Toss the ingredients in the batter.

6. Heat up a wide bottomed pan on the hob (and warm the oven to 200C).

7. Pour in a depth of 1-2 cm of cooking oil in the pan and heat up. Using 2 dessert spoons spoon the mixture into the pan.

8. Lower the heat if cooking too fast but you'll need to let them cook through before turning or they will stick. They should take about 5-7 minutes and you can put them in a hot oven to crisp up and warm through once they are all done.

9. Meanwhile prepare a crisp salad with finely sliced cos lettuce, ½ a cucumber and spring onions. Half fresh lemons. Serve with raita (Page 29).

'CHICKN' CURRY PUFFS

Using the recipe from 'Take-Away Style Ch'cken Curry' (Page 79)

Serves 6

Tools: Knife, Board, Frying pan or wok

Timings: prep 5, cooking 30, total 35 minutes plus cooling time

INGREDIENTS:

- 500g ready-made Puff Pastry baked as per instructions (most packet pastries are vegan).

METHOD:

1. Make up the curry as described on (Page 79)

2. Mix with 2 cups of boiled rice. Use white basmati or try short grain brown rice for a nuttier texture.

3. Cook a sheet of puff pastry as per packet instructions.

4. When it's cool, remove a thick top layer, fill with curry and cut into 6 pieces.

This is delicious party food.

TOFU PITTAS

I'll admit that when I excluded animal products from my diet, initially I wasn't a big fan of tofu. It's incredible how quickly your tastes change as now I really enjoy it in lots of different ways. I don't eat it regularly and certainly not this version, deep fried isn't the healthiest. That said, this is gorgeous! Eaten in a soft fluffy bao-like pitta it's tough to not have 2! It will work in flat-bread, chapatti, pitta or even soft rolls.

Tools: knife / board/ Frying pan

Timings: Prep 10, cooking 5-10, total 20 minutes

INGREDIENTS:

- 1 pack tofu
- 2 tablespoon soy sauce
- 2 tablespoon vegan Worcestershire/ Henderson's sauce
- ½ teaspoon chilli powder or fresh chopped chilli to your taste/ heat
- 1 teaspoon paprika
- 1 tablespoon sesame oil (optional)
- 3 tablespoons nutritional yeast
- A salad of 2 Little gem lettuce/ 100g watercress/ a red pepper/ ½ cucumber/ juice of a fresh lemon or lime/ 1 tablespoon sesame oil.

METHOD:

1. Drain and slice the tofu like a loaf about 1cm wide slices, then slice these into 1.5cm "soldiers". Dry on kitchen paper which will allow the tofu to soak up the marinade.

2. Make a marinade of a soy sauce/ vegan Worcestershire sauce/ fresh chilli or chilli powder/ a teaspoon of paprika or my preference, a teaspoon of smoked paprika with an optional tablespoon of sesame oil and toss and soak the tofu pieces in this while you prepare the salad.

3. Chop a lettuce into thin lengths, add peppery leaves like rocket or watercress, thin strips of red pepper and cucumber and toss this in a tablespoon of lemon juice, lime juice or vinegar and an optional teaspoon of sesame oil.

4. Heat 2 cm depth of oil in a pan. Drain the marinade off the tofu or it will spit when it hits the oil and add it carefully. Keep the marinade.

5. It takes a couple of minutes on high heat to brown and crisp then remove it from the pan. You can keep it warm in a hot oven if you want.

6. Break open the pittas; there is an option here to toast them but if you manage to get these bao-like ones as suggested, I wouldn't bother. You can dip the cut side into the marinade and smear with 2 teaspoons of "veganaise" (vegan mayo).

7. Fill with the lemony-sesame salad, stuff with spiced tofu pieces and enjoy.

SPICEY POTATO WRAPS

This mixture will fill 4 wraps easily, makes a great lunch-time meal and can be enjoyed cold or reheated.

Tools: Knife, Board, Colander, Frying pan or wok

INGREDIENTS:

- 4 medium sized potatoes, normal or sweet variety or a mix of the 2 works equally well
- 1 large onion
- 2 cloves garlic finely chopped
- 1 teaspoon turmeric
- 4 teaspoons garam masala
- 4 tablespoons fresh coriander
- 4 tomatoes
- Tamarind chutney
- 1 lettuce or
- 2 little gem lettuce
- 1 lemon
- Wraps of your choice.
- There are so many delicious varieties: GF, seeded, wholemeal, wholegrain, white, half and half, corn.....

METHOD:

1. Either boil the potatoes, then chop them when soft but not breaking, or cut into 1cm cubes and boil for a shorter time. Drain in a colander and allow to cool.

2. Chop the onion in half and then into thin half-moons and dry fry until the pieces separate and blacken. Add the garam masala, chopped garlic, turmeric and a tablespoon of oil is optional here. Cook the spices for a minute on a low heat. Add half a cup of water, a tablespoon of tamarind chutney and the chopped potatoes. Stir gently as the sauce thickens but so the potatoes don't break up. Taste for salt and pepper. Cook on the hob for a minute.

3. Meanwhile warm your wraps up (oven or microwave), chop the lettuce into strips and squeeze over the juice of the lemon.

4. Chop the tomatoes into 1cm pieces and finely chop the coriander. Turn the heat off, add to the pan and stir through. Pile the spicey potato mix into a warm wrap, top with salad, roll up and enjoy. I smear the wrap with extra tamarind chutney and you could add any spicey sauce.

CHICKPEA 'TUNA'

Tools: Board, fork, knife

Timings: Prep 10 minutes

This will give 2 very generous servings of delicious sandwich filling. This recipe contains a specialty ingredient, Nori seaweed flakes that you might have to make a special effort to find it. It's usually stocked in the big or international supermarkets.

INGREDIENTS:

- 1 tin chickpeas or approximately 300g soaked and cooked chick peas
- 1 tablespoon Nori seaweed sprinkle flakes
- 2 small spring onions
- 1 tablespoon fresh lemon juice
- 2 teaspoons apple cider vinegar
- 1 tablespoon nutritional yeast
- 2 tablespoons vegan mayonnaise
- Salt and pepper

METHOD:

1. Finely chop the spring onions and soak in the vinegar and lemon juice.

2. Drain and squash the chick peas on the board with a fork.

3. Sprinkle with a tablespoon of the nori flakes, nutritional yeast, ½ teaspoon sea salt, black pepper.

4. Scrape into the bowl with the spring onions, add the mayo and mix well. Taste and adjust seasoning if needed.

This can be served on sandwiches with peppery rocket or watercress salad and pickled beetroot. Or it can be mixed in with cold pasta and a tin of sweetcorn or just enjoyed from the bowl.

FALAFEL WRAPS

Tools: Knife, board, blender or potato masher, frying pan

Timings: Prep 10 minutes, cooking 5 minutes, total 15 minutes

Makes 2 portions. Of course you can use shop bought ready-made falafels.

INGREDIENTS:

- 1 tin of prepared chick peas or soak your own.
- ½ finely chopped red or brown onion, precook if you don't like raw onion.
- ½ teaspoon garlic salt or crushed garlic
- ½ teaspoon salt
- Sprinkle black pepper
- 1 teaspoon cumin
- 1 tablespoon chopped coriander
- 2 tablespoons flour (chick-pea or plain)

To serve:

- Flatbreads, wraps or chapatti.
- 1 Baby gem lettuce
- ½ jar of sundried tomatoes
- 2 tablespoons hummus
- 1 lemon

METHOD:

1. Fry the onions for 5 minutes in a tablespoon of oil or water until they cook a little. Blend or mash everything together, then shape into 6 balls. Roll in flour or fine bread crumbs for extra crunch, and fry for 6 minutes, turning after 2 minutes. You can squash the balls into flat patties or cook them in a deep fat fryer.

2. I love them served in a wrap slathered in hummus, topped with chopped sundried tomatoes and baby gem lettuce, squirted generously with fresh lemon.

PULL-YOUR-LEG 'PORK' ROLLS

Toooooo yummie. We love this in 'tiger' French bread for an extra bite.

Makes 6 generously loaded buns.

Tools: knife/ board/ Large pan/ grater/ bowl

INGREDIENTS:

- 2 tins of jackfruit
- 1 large carrot
- Bottle of shop bought BBQ sauce

BBQ seasoning

- 1 tablespoon brown sugar,
- 2 teaspoons paprika,
- 1 teaspoon garlic powder,
- 1 teaspoon salt,
- 1 teaspoon chilli powder and
- ½ teaspoon black pepper.
-

For the Slaw:

- See Page 41

METHOD:

1. I can only find tinned jackfruit in salted water so I soak it first for an hour or so. You can miss out this step if yours tastes ok. Drain the jackfruit and grate the hard central stalks until you reach the 'strandy' bits. These will break up on their own during cooking to create the stringy effect of pulled pork.

2. Grate a large carrot and add this to the jackfruit.

3. Make the BBQ seasoning and rub it into the jackfruit and carrot. Leave to absorb the flavours for 10 minutes.

4. This BBQ mix is personal- more sugar/ more chilli/ less salt.... Do any variation that suits.

5. Now make the slaw (Page 41)

6. Take a large frying pan and add a tablespoon of vegetable oil. When hot, pop the marinating jackfruit carrot mix in and brown slightly at a high heat as the sugar caramelises. Keep stirring for a few minutes then add a cup of BBQ sauce and 4 tablespoons of water. Simmer gently until the jackfruit flesh breaks up and the carrots are softened. It takes a good 10 minutes and you may need to add water or more BBQ sauce.

7. Break it up using 2 forks, pulling at the strands. Taste. It should be stickily sweet yet tangy and spicy.

8. Break open a tiger bun, pile with pull-your-leg-pork and heap on the slaw.

9. Grab a napkin or plate to catch the bits ... Truly dirty vegan.

HUMMUS

Shop bought hummus is an easy go-to for toast, as a dip for chopped raw veg, or with tortilla wraps but this version is quick and easy and you can mess about with the seasonings to your own taste.

Tools: Knife/ board/ blender/grater

Timings: Total 10 minutes

INGREDIENTS:

- 1 tin chickpeas or soaked and cooked chick peas
- 1 clove chopped and squashed garlic with ½ teaspoon salt (optional) Or ½ teaspoon garlic powder
- ½ teaspoon paprika
- 1 tablespoon olive oil (optional)
- 1 tablespoon tahini

METHOD:

1. Zest and juice a large fresh lemon.

2. Open a tin of chick peas, keep the juice and put the peas in a blender.

3. Add half the chopped clove of garlic, which you have softened and squashed in the salt.

4. Add a teaspoon of paprika, a tablespoon of olive oil (optional), a tablespoon of tahini and the juice of a large lemon with or without the zest.

5. Whizz until smooth but there should still be a texture. Taste and add salt and pepper if you prefer.

6. Add chick pea water until you get a good thick dipping consistency- I find I need half the water but it does depend on the chick pea tin.

7. Prepare your 'crudites' by chopping raw broccoli, cauliflower, peppers, cucumber, carrot, celery, corn crisps (tortillas) and maybe toast or bread sticks.

HOLY GUACAMOLE

This will make a bowl, enough for a dip or as a side to fajitas for 4-6 people

Tools: knife/ board/ bowl/grater or zester

Timings: Prep 10 minutes

INGREDIENTS:

- 3 ripe tomatoes
- 1 red onion or 3 spring onions
- 1 or 2 fresh chillies
- Zest and juice of 2 limes
- 3 tablespoons apple cider vinegar
- 3 ripe avocados (I don't drive but I av-a-car-doh)
- 1 tablespoon chopped fresh or frozen coriander
- Salt and Pepper (optional to taste)

METHOD:

1. Chop 3 ripe tomatoes into small pieces, same with a red onion and fresh chilli.

2. I would use 2 bird's eye chillies but this is very much a personal taste.

3. Add the zest and juice of 2 limes (I grate them on the block grater fine side to get the dark green skin off) and 3 tablespoons of apple cider vinegar.

4. Put all these ingredients in a bowl and leave to soak. I find it takes the harshness out of the onion which I don't like as I can't eat raw onion so you might want to omit this step.

5. Chop 3 ripe avocados, finely chop a handful of fresh coriander and add this to the tomato mix. Salt and pepper to taste.

SALSA

This will make a bowl, enough for a dip or as a side to fajitas for 4-6 people

Tools: Board, knife, bowl, box grater

Timings: Prep 10, resting 60 if available. Total 70 minutes

INGREDIENTS:

- 4 ripe tomatoes
- ½ red onion
- 4 tablespoons apple cider vinegar
- 2-3 chillies
- 1 tablespoon fresh coriander
- Zest and juice of 3 limes
- Salt and Pepper

METHOD:

1. Chop the onion very finely and soak in the vinegar. Add the chopped chilli and finely chopped tomatoes (you can grate these instead if you prefer)

2. Zest the limes on the fine side of a box grater and add this as well as the juice of the limes.

3. Chop the coriander, add and stir well. Add salt and pepper to taste and leave for an hour for the flavours to mix.

RAITA

Tools: board, knife, bowl

Timings: Prep 10 minutes

INGREDIENTS:

- 1 cup yogurt (I prefer coconut)
- 1/2 teaspoon garam masala
- 1/3 cucumber, seeds removed and grated
- Handful of fresh mint and coriander, finely chopped
- The zest grated and juice squeezed from ½ lime

METHOD:

1. Chop and grate all the ingredients as described
2. Add to a bowl, taste for salt and pepper
3. Top with a few fresh herbs.

SALADS

SIMPLE SALAD

No rules here. Just a simple, quick, easy accompaniment to a meal for 4 or topped with nuts and seeds to make a complete meal. In the words of Dr Klaper, an internationally recognised teacher on diet and health, "If someone doesn't comment on the size of your salad, it's not big enough".

Tools: Knife, board

Timings: Prep 10 minutes

INGREDIENTS:

- 1 lettuce (iceberg, cos, 2 little gems, any other leaves)
- 1 cucumber
- 4 tomatoes
- Good options to add: Avocado, beetroot, watercress, grated carrot, grapefruit, peaches, herbs.

METHOD:

1. Chop into bite sized pieces and dress with Fresh lime juice

Or

2. Tahini dressing made from a tablespoon of tahini, 2 tablespoons of water, 1 tablespoon of fresh lemon juice and black pepper mixed together.

BEANEY SALAD

Easy peasy tinny!

Feeds 2

Tools: Bowl/ knife/ board

Timings: Prep 10 minutes

INGREDIENTS:

- 1 tin or box of cooked cannellini beans, or soak and cook your own
- 1 tin sweetcorn
- ½ a cucumber
- 4 tomatoes
- 4 spring onions
- 1 red pepper
- 1 tablespoon olive oil
- 1 crushed clove of garlic
- 2 tablespoons of finely chopped coriander and parsley
- Juice of 1 lemon
- Salt and Pepper

METHOD:

1. Open a tin of cannellini beans and drain. Same with a tin of sweetcorn.

2. Chop half a cucumber, 4 tomatoes, 4 spring onions and a red pepper and add to the bowl.

3. Make a dressing with a tablespoon olive oil, a crushed clove of garlic, a handful each of finely chopped coriander and parsley, salt and pepper and the juice of a lemon.

4. Pour over, stir and taste!

SATISFYING SPICEY SALAD

Tools: knife, board, bowl

Timings: Prep 10, cooking 8, total 18 minutes

INGREDIENTS for 2:

- 1 lettuce (cos/ iceberg or a soft leaf variety)
- 1 cucumber
- 4 tomatoes
- 2 avocados (optional)
- 1 tablespoon sunflower seeds
- 1 tablespoon pumpkin seeds
- 1 lime
- 1 tablespoon apple cider vinegar
- ½ jar sunblush tomatoes (optional)
- 50g your favourite olives (optional)
- 200g chestnut mushrooms or tofu or tempeh
- 1 chilli
- 4 cloves garlic finely chopped
- Maggi maggi sauce, salt and pepper

METHOD:

1. Slice the mushrooms and heat in 2 tablespoons water on a high heat. If the mushrooms start to stick keep adding a spoon of water.

2. Once the mushrooms are softened, add the finely chopped chilli and garlic, a tablespoon of vegetable oil if you wish and cook for a minute before adding a tablespoon of maggi-maggi sauce. You can substitute a teaspoon of yeast spread or soy sauce if you don't have maggi-maggi sauce. Add salt and pepper and turn the heat off.

3. Make the salad by chopping the lettuce long ways first then cutting into strips. If you de-seed the cucumber which makes the salad less watery, make sure you eat this nutritious part.

4. Chop the cucumber and tomatoes, avocado and put them in a bowl.

5. Chop any optional extras; I like sundried or sunblush tomatoes, olives, gherkins, beetroot......

6. Grate the zest of a lime over it, squeeze the juice of the lime, a tablespoon of apple cider vinegar and the mushrooms and toss with your fingers.

7. Sprinkle with the seeds if you have them and enjoy this slightly warm salad. Option to have a bread roll to mop up any mushroomy juices.

8. If you don't like mushrooms, make the salad and replace the mushrooms with tofu or tempeh.

THAI GREEN PAPAYA OR WHITE CABBAGE SALAD

This delicious, clean tasting and spicey salad can be enjoyed on its own or as part of a starter or accompaniment to your Thai food. If you can't get green papaya I have substituted white cabbage with equally good results. Our international supermarkets in Liverpool normally stock Thai green papaya. This will feed 6-8 people.

Tools: knife, board, grater, bowl

Timings: Prep 20 minutes

INGREDIENTS:

- 2 green papayas or ½ a white cabbage
- 4 large cloves garlic
- 2 tablespoons soy sauce
- 5-10 birdseye chillies
- 4 tablespoons peanuts
- 4 tomatoes
- 150g green beans
- 150g beansprouts (optional)
- 1 ½ tablespoons brown sugar (optional)
- 2-4 limes, zest grated and juice added
- 2 tablespoons coriander (optional)
- 2 tablespoons mint (optional)

METHOD:

1. Grate the papayas or cabbage changing the blade for odd shapes if you wish.

2. Slice the raw green beans in half and in to thirds.

3. Mix this together with the chopped tomatoes and beansprouts.

4. Chop the garlic, chillies and zest the limes and mix this with the soy, lime juice and herbs and pour over the salad.

5. You can add more chillies if it doesn't have enough kick!

THAI CORN SALAD

Tools: Pan, knife, board, box grater, bowl

Timings: Prep 10, cooking 4, total 14 minutes

INGREDIENTS:

- 4 corn on the cobs
- 100g green beans, sliced in half and cut into 3
- 100g tomatoes
- 1 large carrot, grated
- 4 cloves garlic
- 2 tablespoons peanuts, dry roasted in a hot pan.
- 2 tablespoons fresh lime juice
- 2 tablespoons soy sauce
- 2 teaspoons brown sugar (optional)
- 5-10 birdseye chillies

METHOD:

1. Boil the corns for 4 minutes and plunge into ice cold water for 2 minutes.

2. Holding the corns end-on, slice chunks of corn kernels off the cob.

3. Add the chopped tomatoes, grated carrot and green beans.

4. Finely chop and crush the garlic, chillies and nuts and add to the lime juice, soy sauce and optional sugar.

5. Taste and add more lime juice or chilli if you wish before coating the corn salad in it. It's often better to use your hands to get all the flavours into every part of the dish.

RED CABBAGE SLAW

Makes 6 portions

Tools: knife/ board/ Large pan/ grater/ bowl.

INGREDIENTS:

- ½ red cabbage
- 2 carrots
- ½ red onion
- 3 tablespoons apple cider vinegar
- 4 tablespoons soya free veganaise/ vegan mayonnaise
- 1 cup pumpkin seeds
- Juice of a lemon

METHOD:

1. Grate the carrots and red cabbage.

2. Chop the red onion into really small pieces and soak in the vinegar for about 5-10 minutes.

3. Put these ingredients all in a bowl and add 4 large tablespoons of veganaise, the lemon juice and the pumpkin seeds and stir to mix well.

4. Taste to see if it needs salt/ pepper or more lemon juice.

SOUPS

CELERIAC AND CHESTNUT SOUP

Try it to believe how good it is!

Tools: knife/ board/ pan/ blender

Timings: Prep 10, cooking 30, total 40 minutes

INGREDIENTS:

- 2 celery sticks
- 1 Large onion
- 2 carrots
- 1 celeriac weighing approx. 500g (celeriac is the hard, knobbly base of the celery plant)
- 2 litres stock (I use low salt vegan bouillon)
- 1 Packet of peeled chestnuts around 200g normally (these can be tinned or vacuum packed and are often on sale after Christmas, or you can buy tins of chestnut puree).

METHOD:

1. Finely chop 2 celery sticks an onion and 2 carrots. Put them in the pan with 2 tablespoons of oil or water and put on the heat. Stir till they start to warm through then put the lid on and let them sweat.

2. Chop the celeriac, a round, ugly, nobly veg that, like the butternut squash is another hard one I'm afraid. Add your hard earned chunks to the pan when you've finished it all as the other veg should be softened.

3. Add 2 litres of veggie stock (I use low salt vegan bouillon).

4. Boil gently for 20-30 minutes until the celeriac is softened then add a vacuum pack of peeled chestnuts.

5. Warm through for 2 minutes then blend until it is beautifully silky smooth.

6. Season with salt and pepper to your taste.

7. Option to drizzle a tiny amount of flavoured oil on top to make it ooze professional grace.

CREAMY BUTTERNUT SOUP

This is a rich, creamy, smooth soup that's filling too,

Tools: knife/ board/ pan/ blender

Timings: Prep 10, cooking 20, total 30 minutes

INGREDIENTS:

- Butternut Squash (weight approximately 500g/ 1lb)
- 2 celery sticks
- 1 Large onion
- 2 carrots
- 1 Tin coconut milk
- 2 tablespoons Thai curry paste
- 2 litres vegetable stock (Vegan low salt vegetable bouillion)

METHOD:

1. Finely chop 2 celery sticks, an onion and 2 carrots. Put them in the pan with 2 tablespoons of oil or water and put on the heat. Stir till they start to warm through then put the lid on and let them sweat.

2. Chop a butternut squash. There is an option to microwave it for 2 minutes first to make it softer and therefore easier or just expend some energy. I slice from the top in sections crossways then remove the seeds from inside as I come across them and when it's all chopped, add to the pan. Stir 2 tablespoons of Thai or Vietnamese curry paste into the vegetables and cook for a minute.

3. Make up 2 litres of veggie stock (I use vegan low salt bouillon powder) and add to the soup. When it comes to a rolling boil reduce the heat and simmer for 15 minutes until the squash is soft.

4. Add a tin of coconut milk if you like and season with salt and pepper to your taste. Blend until uber smooth and creamy.

Options:

5. You can leave out the curry paste, it still gorgeous.

6. Add grated fresh ginger and turmeric. (1-2 inch pieces)

LENTIL SOUP

Easy, warming soup feeds 4 with leftovers for the next day.

Tools: large pan / Knife/ board

Timings: Prep 10, cooking 30, total 40 minutes

INGREDIENTS:

- 250g red lentils
- 4 large carrots
- 4 sticks celery
- 1 large onion or a bunch of spring onions
- 2 litres of vegetable stock (I add 2 tablespoons vegan low salt bouillon to 4 pints water)

METHOD:

1. Add the lentils and water to a large pan and bring it to a rolling boil. Stir and leave while you chop the onion, 4 large carrots, 4 sticks of celery. Add these to the pan, reduce the heat and simmer for 20 minutes. The lentils will plump up.

2. Add a tablespoon of vegan bouillon for every litre of water, normally 2 litres for my pan but taste it as some are saltier than others.

3. Add lots of black pepper. Serve with spring onion chopped on top and a hunk of bread next to it.

4. Added flavour option: Add a bulb of garlic, 2 inches fresh ginger chopped or grated and 2 inches fresh turmeric or 2 teaspoons powdered turmeric.

5. Dirty vegan option: crispy fry some vegan bacon ('cheatin' range tastes like the real thing) or seaweed 'bacon' and add on top.

MINESTRONE SOUP

Tools: knife/ board/ pan

Timings: Prep 10, cooking 20, total 30 minutes

INGREDIENTS:

- 3 celery sticks
- 1 onion
- 3 cloves of garlic
- 3 carrots
- 2 red peppers
- Olive oil (optional)
- 2 tins chopped tomatoes
- Vegan low salt bouillon powder
- Tomato puree
- Salt and black pepper
- Tin of cannellini beans
- Flat leaf parsley

METHOD:

1. Finely chop 3 celery sticks, an onion, 3 cloves of garlic and 3 carrots. Put them in the pan with 2 tablespoons of oil or water and put on the heat. Stir until they start to warm through then put the lid on and let them sweat for 5 minutes, giving the occasional stir to make sure it doesn't stick to the bottom of the pan.

2. Add 2 tins of chopped tomatoes, 2 tins of water, a tablespoon of vegan bouillon powder, 2 tablespoons of tomato puree and loads of black pepper. When it comes to a rolling boil reduce the heat and simmer for 15 minutes.

3. Drain a tin of cannellini beans and add them to the soup.

4. Finely chop a handful of flat leaf parsley to sprinkle on top when you've ladled it out chunkily into your bowl.

5. Option to sprinkle with your favourite cheese.

ROSE RED PEPPER & HARISSA SOUP

This soup has a tomatoey chilli kick and the kitchen smells of those delicious charred peppers.

TOOLS: Knife/ board/ saucepan/ stick blender or other blender or no blender if you like a chunky texture.

Timings: Prep 10, cooking 40, total 50 minutes

INGREDIENTS:

- 3 red peppers
- 3 carrots
- 1 onion
- 2 potatoes
- 4 celery sticks
- 1 chilli
- 4 cloves garlic
- 2 teaspoons rose harissa
- 2 tins tomatoes
- 2 tablespoons tomato puree

METHOD:

1. Blacken the peppers.

2. I have a gas hob to do this on- keep turning the peppers every 20 seconds till the skin blackens and blisters, then put them aside to cool.

3. An alternative is to put them in a really hot oven for 20 minutes directly onto the rungs with a tray beneath.

4. Chop the potatoes, carrots, onion, celery and peppers into 1cmx 1cm pieces but no need for exact precision here, half the chilli and add this. For the garlic: chop finely and crush with the flat of a knife or crush with ½ teaspoon salt.

5. Add all the veg, tinned tomatoes, tomato puree and rose harissa to the saucepan, bring to the boil then lower the heat and simmer for 20mins. I use a stick blender to blend the soup then taste to check for seasoning. Salt and pepper as you wish, maybe add extra slithers of fresh red chilli and serve warm with garlic bread.

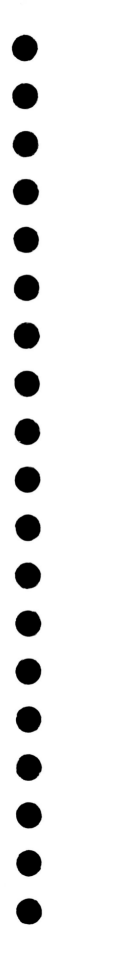

BREAKFASTS

BREAKFAST OPTIONS

For most of my working life I enjoyed two breakfasts, a bit like a Hobbit, one on wakening and another at half-ten/ eleven. When I was a hospital doctor, this would mean breakfast at home around 7 and another in between the morning ward round and going to theatre, or ordering breakfast butties from the canteen to our clinic rooms. As a GP I was a firm believer that a big breakfast was the right start to the day and I would think a 3 egg omelette was a great start, but it doesn't suit me now and it isn't healthy. If you prolong the time from waking to when you break-the-fast, you may find it suits you better.

For me, water and fruit or a smoothie loaded with fruit and cacao powder is a great start and I might snack on raw veggies or fruit at some point in the morning. If I'm out walking the dogs I might have beans and mushrooms on toast around 10.30. It changes, there is no rule. If you are overweight less calories is always going to work in your favour and resting your body by fasting it, drinking only water or eating whole fruits and having a later breakfast may also be beneficial.

If you are going to have breakfast it's an opportunity to set your intentions for the day with this meal. You should feel happy that you are eating and feeding your body, showing it love and be thankful for the food we have to eat and the opportunity to be together if we share our morning meal with others.

AVOCADO

Smash an avocado on a piece of toast. Option to add a sprinkle of chilli flakes, salt, pepper, chopped coriander leaves and a squirt of lime.

PORRIDGE

I love whole oats made with a plant based milk (almond has the least calories with all the nutrients but oat is my current favourite). I grate in a red apple and a teaspoon of mixed spice to a cup of oats with 2 cups of milk. Bring it to a slow simmer, stirring and adding more milk if needed.

Sprinkle with mixed chopped nuts when it's cooked if you wish and you won't be hungry till lunchtime. You can make this with a tin of coconut milk for a really creamy porridge topped with bananas, nuts and drizzled with date syrup.

SMOOTHIE

I have a nutribullet-like blender to make these; just remember to wash it as soon as you have finished.

My base is 2 bananas, a cup of water, coconut, oat or almond milk and then I add either

- A cup of Frozen berries, 2 tablespoons cacao.
- A frozen avocado half, 2 cubes frozen spinach and an optional teaspoon spirulina.
- A large handful of kale, half a mango or cup of frozen mango.

Blend and enjoy or pour into a screw-top jar to take to work.

If the smoothie is very thick pop it in a bowl and add colourful toppings like fruit, nuts and seeds and enjoy it like a frozen dessert.

CHIA PUDDINGS

These tiny black nutritious seeds soak up any liquid they are added to and create a thick, delicious, bobbly, dessert-like texture which is lovely topped with fresh fruit. I like mine soaked in oat milk but any plant milk or water is fine.

MUESLI

My current favourite is £1 from Iceland, but Lizzie's sugar free one is delicious too with lots of texture. I have it with a chopped banana and lots of plant-based milk.

THE FULL WORKS

For the crème de le crème of brekkies I make my own baked beans to accompany shop bought vegan sausages and vegan black pudding. Fry up mushrooms and tomatoes and serve with toast topped with vegan butter or avocado.

GLUTEN FREE

BAKED BEANS

Makes 2 generous portions

Tools: Pan/spoon

INGREDIENTS:

- A tin of cannellini or black beans
- A tablespoon of tomato puree
- Henderson's vegan 'worcestershire' sauce
- Salt and pepper
- A tablespoon of water

METHOD:

1. Drain a tin of cannellini or black beans, add a tablespoon of tomato puree, Henderson's vegan 'worcestershire' sauce, salt and pepper and heat gently in a pan on the hob, stirring so it doesn't stick and maybe adding a tablespoon of water if needed to loosen. I suppose it depends how you like the sauce on your beans.

2. You can add chopped onion, garlic, chopped tomatoes, mushrooms or anything really to this. I like some bird eye chilli for a mid-morning snack.

TOFU SCRAMBLE

Tools: Bowl, pan, spatula

INGREDIENTS:

- 1 block tofu or box of silken tofu
- 1 teaspoon turmeric
- 1 tablespoon nutritional yeast
- Salt and pepper optional black salt (specialty ingredient that smells like egg, the same sulphurous, stink bomb odour).
- Optional chopped chilli, coriander, ½ teaspoon cumin or 4 teaspoons harissa spice mix.

METHOD:

1. Heat the pan, crumble the tofu between your fingers and add it to the bowl with the other ingredients. I like it spicey and enjoy the chilli kick so I add the cumin and chopped chilli.

2. Add a tablespoon of water to the hot pan and then the tofu mix. Stir until it is heated through and serve warm.

3. This is nice as part of a breakfast or served on toast.

OATY WHOLEMEAL PANCAKES

Tools: Pan, spatula or 'fish'-slice to flip pancakes, bowl, whisk

This mix will serve 2-4 people. It's easy to make more should you have a hungry crowd and equally it will keep covered in the fridge for a day.

It can also be made without oats and with self-raising flour to make a more traditionally textured pancake.

INGREDIENTS:

- 1 cup wholemeal flour
- 1/2 cup porridge oats
- 1 teaspoon baking powder
- 1 teaspoon ground mixed spice
- 1-2 cups plant milk (I prefer oat but soy, almond, coconut all work)
- 1 tablespoon icing sugar (optional)
- 2 tablespoons oil (I prefer coconut)

METHOD:

1. Add the flour, oats, baking powder, melted oil and 1 cup milk to the bowl and whisk. It needs to be well beaten and be a dropping consistency, not too thick and not too thin, unless you want to make crepes in which case thin is good and this recipe works well for both. Add more milk if needed.

2. Heat up a 6-8 inch frying pan and add a smear of oil. For American pancakes put 4 large tablespoons of the batter in the pan. Wait a minute and a half ish or until you see plenty of bubbles coming through to the wet batter surface before turning. If these look 'over-brown' lower the heat.

3. If making crepes the first one will reliably be awful. Keep the pan lightly oiled and add about 2 tablespoons of batter. Roll around the pan to form a thin layer. As the edges crisp and separate from the edge of the pan, use a spatula to turn it and cook the other side briefly.

4. These pancakes are delicious with sweet or savoury toppings and I think they get better cold. They can be warm, sugarless and a great base for a mushroom filling or they can be truly dirty vegan, stacked American style, topped with fruit and dripping in syrup.

MEALS

EASY PASTA SAUCE

This pasta sauce is red, coats any pasta, is simple to make and is packed with nutritious veg, all hidden. It will serve 4 easily.

Tools: Large pan, knife, board and the all-important blender

Prepartion 5 minutes, cooking 10 minutes, total 15 minutes

INGREDIENTS:

- 1 large onion
- 3 sticks celery
- 3 carrots
- Other optional veg include 2 courgettes, 2 peppers.
- 1 tin tomatoes
- 3 tablespoons tomato puree
- Optional 2 cloves of garlic, chopped, a teaspoon of Italian seasoning.

METHOD:

1. Chop the vegetables roughly the same size and heat in a pan with a cup of water.

2. Add a tin of tomatoes and 3 tablespoons of tomato puree. Heat, stir and taste.

3. Cook the vegetables down for 8 minutes, remove from the heat and blend. I use a stick blender but any will do. Taste again.

4. This can be used as a pizza topper as well as pasta sauce.

PASTA BOLOGNAISE

Tools: Large pan, knife, board

Preparation 10 minutes, cooking 15 minutes, total 25 minutes

INGREDIENTS:

- 1 red pepper
- 1 green pepper
- 200g mushrooms
- 1 large onion
- 4 cloves garlic chopped and crushed in ½ tablespoon salt
- 2 teaspoons Italian seasoning
- 1 tin brown lentils
- 2 tins chopped tomatoes
- 2 tablespoons tomato puree
- Salt and black pepper
- Pasta for 4 any shape you like

METHOD:

1. Chop the onions and peppers, and place in a large pan with the garlic and 4 tablespoons water, boil and stir rapidly.

2. After 2 mins add the chopped mushrooms and more water if it is all boiled off.

3. Add a tablespoon of optional maggi maggi sauce and after a minute add the herbs, tomato puree, tomatoes, lentils and boil for 5 minutes.

4. Taste for seasoning and simmer with the lid on for 5 more then turn off the heat if the veggies are soft.

5. Cook the pasta as it says on the packet in a large pan of boiling water. It can be anything from 2-14 minutes. Drain and smother in the sauce.

6. There are many plant based cheese available if you wish to try them sprinkled on top.

MUSHROOM PASTA

Serves 4

Tools: Knife / board/ 2 pans

Preparation 5 minutes, cook 25 minutes, total 30 minutes

INGREDIENTS:

- 1 onion
- 1 tablespoon oil
- 4 cloves of garlic, finely chopped
- 400g mushrooms
- 1 tablespoon cornflour
- 1 tablespoon vegetable bouillon
- 500mls plant based milk (I like oat)
- 2 tablespoons nutritional yeast (optional)
- Salt and Pepper
- 2 tablespoons chopped flat leaf parsley
- 500g pasta (whole-wheat, white, spelt, gluten-free.....)

METHOD:

1. Chop an onion and fry on a low heat in 2 tablespoons oil.

2. Add 4 cloves of finely chopped garlic and put the lid on the pan to let it sweat.

3. Slice a large pack of mushrooms or 2 smaller ones of different types. I like chestnut ones for flavour and texture but any are fine.

4. Add to the pan and put the lid back on for 5 minutes.

5. Add a tablespoon of cornflour and a tablespoon of vegan bouillon to 500mls of a plant based milk.

6. Add this to the mushrooms and stir while it thickens. Add the nutritional yeast if using.

7. Add lots of black pepper. Taste if it needs salt.

8. Heat a large pan of water to a rolling boil and add a packet of pasta.

9. Finely chop a handful of flat leaved parsley.

10. Drain the pasta once it's cooked and add to the sauce or mix each portion as you go, sprinkle with parsley and twirl it up on your fork!

MUSHROOM RISOTTO

Serves 4.

Using the dried mushrooms, soaking them and adding the water to the stock really adds flavour and is worthwhile if you can find them in your local shop.

Tools: Knife/ board/ large wide-bottomed pan

Prep5 cook 25 total 30 minutes

INGREDIENTS:

- 2 cups of risotto rice
- 1 large onion
- 4 cloves garlic, finely chopped
- 2 teaspoons fresh or dried thyme or sage
- 250g fresh mushrooms and 2 tablespoons of dried mushrooms (mixed or porcin, often found in a specialty section in the shops)
- Vegetable stock; I use 4 teaspoons bouillon made up to 600mls but taste for saltiness
- 100mls soya cream
- Fresh flat leaf parsley
- Salt and black pepper

METHOD:

1. Soak 2 tablespoons of dried mixed or porcini mushrooms in a cup of boiled water for 30 minutes or longer.

2. Finely chop an onion and 4 cloves of garlic and fry on a low heat in 2 tablespoons of olive oil for a few minutes. Watch as the onion becomes clearer/ translucent before adding the risotto rice and the edges of this will also change but don't let either burn. Sprinkle some fresh or dried thyme or sage into the pan, whichever you prefer the smell of.

3. Chop 250g of any fresh mushrooms (I like chestnut ones) and add them to the pan. Drain the soaking mushrooms but keep the juice, chop the rehydrated mushrooms and add them.

4. Make up a veggie stock in a jug with 4 teaspoons of vegan bouillon in 600mls of boiled water and add the mushroom juice if you have it.

5. Stir the risotto, adding the liquid slowly, meditatively over the next 15 minutes until the rice is cooked. Keep checking after 10 minutes for the texture and wetness you prefer.

6. Add some soya cream, lots of black pepper and 2 handfuls of finely chopped flat leaf parsley. Taste check!

7. Serve with a salad: Chop an iceberg lettuce, 4 tomatoes, half a cucumber to a bowl and maybe half a bag of fresh spinach leaves also chopped. Dress by squeezing over with the juice of a fresh lemon or lime.

BAKED AUBERGINES

Serves 2-4 depending on size of the aubergines.

Tools: Board/ knife/ baking tray/ pan/ oven proof dish

Preparation 10 minutes, cooking 60 minutes, total 70 minutes

INGREDIENTS:

- 2 aubergines
- 1 whole bulb garlic
- 4 tablespoons olive oil
- 1 onion
- 1 tablespoon tomato puree
- 1 tin chopped tomatoes
- Optional grated cheese/ sheese/ cheese

METHOD:

1. Cut an aubergine in half and score a criss cross pattern in the flesh. Lay one or 2 aubergines like this in a baking tray.

2. Slice fresh garlic and push this into the criss/crosses. Pour over 4 tablespoons of oil, cover or wrap in foil and bake in the oven at 180 degrees until soft, check after 40 minutes.

3. Chop an onion and fry it in a tablespoon of oil.

4. Add 2 cloves of finely chopped fresh garlic and cook for a minute with the lid on.

5. Add a tablespoon of tomato puree, a tin of tomatoes and simmer gently for about 10minutes. The sauce will become rich and thick. Place the cooked aubergine on an ovenproof plate, pour the tomato sauce over, top with grated vegan cheese and bake in the oven or under the grill for 10 minutes more.

6. Serve a portion of this with a salad: chop a lettuce/ 4 tomatoes/ half a cucumber and sprinkle with the juice of half a lemon.

7. Have a wholegrain bread roll to soak up the sauce.

PIZZAS

I hope you do this and realise pizza dough is easy to make; it takes just 15 minutes of therapeutic pounding to create a delicious, satisfying dough that you can flavour if you like and shape however you want. Great for kids, these are healthy and fun to prepare. This makes 6 bases.

Tools: Large bowl/ sieve/ baking trays/ blender

INGREDIENTS:

- 600g strong white, wholemeal, seeded or bread flour
- Teaspoon salt
- 14g dried yeast
- 3 tablespoons oil
- 375ml warm water
- 1 tablespoon date syrup (optional)

METHOD:

1. Sieve the flour into a large bowl with the salt.

2. Mix the liquid ingredients up with the yeast and add to the flour.

3. Mix it all together and bring it to a ball.

4. Tip this onto a floured surface and knead. Kneading is a personal exercise. It can be one or 2 handed. It can involve pounding and stretching the dough always returning it to a ball shape before going again. Do this for 10minutes. Watch a video if you are unsure.

5. After 10 minutes the dough should feel different, smooth and stretchy. Place it back in the bowl, cover with a damp tea towel (wet a clean tea towel under a warm tap, squeeze out the excess water, then place over the bowl) and leave in a warm place. Most kitchens are warm enough to activate the yeast.

6. After an hour the dough will have risen to at least twice the size and the smell is amazing.

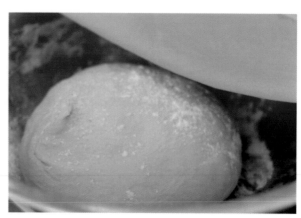

PIZZA SAUCE

INGREDIENTS:

- 1 tin chopped tomatoes
- 1 onion finely chopped
- 2 tablespoons tomato puree
- 2 cloves garlic, chopped
- 1 teaspoon dried Italian seasoning

METHOD:

1. Prepare the sauce by combining the tinned tomatoes, tomato puree, garlic and Italian seasoning in a pan.

2. Heat gently for 5 minutes then blend to a smooth consistency. This makes the pizza topping.

3. Other toppings depend on what you like and what you normally have. I use vegan cheese and I prefer the greek style feta grated on top but there is mozzarella and cheddar varieties available. Slice 1 red pepper and 1 yellow pepper into strips, toss in a little oil and bake in a low oven for 10 minutes to soften the peppers. Put the toppings out so everyone can help themselves. Include 200g sliced mushrooms, 1 tin drained sweetcorn, defrosted spinach cubes, olives, tomatoes ... Anything you fancy. The BBQ jackfruit (Page 22) works really well as a BBQ topping option and if you choose one of: 1 pack of tofu, tempeh, butternut squash or aubergine, cubed and marinated in 1 tablespoon miso, 2 tablespoons water, 1 tablespoon tomato puree, 1 tablespoon soy sauce then roast in the oven for 20 minutes, these little cubes burst with flavour and add a different texture.

4. All your usual toppings will work but steer towards vegetables.

MAKING PIZZA

1. Divide the dough into 6 and roll out each piece. You can shape and press it out on a floured surface with your hands if you don't have a rolling pin. Experiment with thick and thin bases and place on a baking tray before adding the toppings.

2. Go light on the sauce and toppings initially as it allows the dough to rise in the oven and gives a lighter, fluffier base. You can always add more topping but a soggy dough isn't enjoyable.

3. Splash with olive oil and sprinkle with black pepper and cook on 220-240 degrees C in the oven for 8-10 minutes then remove from the tray and place directly on the rack for a further 3 minutes.

FAJITAS

I love the meal experience of making fajitas with bowls of colourful fillings to choose from. This filling will feed 4 people.

Tools: knife/ board/ large frying pan.

Preparation 10 minutes, cooking 10 minutes, total 20minutes

INGREDIENTS:

- 1large onion
- 1 red pepper
- 1 green pepper
- 1 yellow pepper
- 4 large Portobello mushrooms
- 1 tablespoon coconut oil
- 2 teaspoons Cajun spine seasoning
- 2 cloves of garlic, crushed
- 1 tablespoon tomato puree
- 1 tin black beans
- ½ tin chopped tomatoes
- Sat and Pepper
- Optional 1 tablespoon fresh coriander

METHOD:

1. Chop a large onion, a red pepper, a green pepper, a yellow pepper, 4 portobello mushrooms into strips and fry in the large pan with a tablespoon of oil. Stir fry i.e. fry on high heat and keep stirring! The peppers will start to soften after a few minutes.

2. Add a sprinkle of salt/ pepper/ 2 teaspoons Cajun spice seasoning and 2 cloves of chopped garlic and cook for a minute.

3. Add half a tin of chopped tomatoes and more of needed, a tablespoon of tomato puree, drained tin of black beans and simmer for 5 minutes. Stir in a handful of chopped, fresh coriander

4. Taste the veg for spice and texture.

5. Heat a pack of wraps up in the oven.

6. Place bowls of guacamole (Page 27), a bag of fresh chopped spinach, your fajita mix, grated vegan cheese, natural plant-based yogurt and extra chillies on the table.

7. Make a salad using a chopped lettuce, 4 tomatoes and half a cucumber sprinkled with the juice of half a lemon.

8. Place all these on the table and have fun filling the wraps! Have a napkin handy!

CHILLI SIN CARNE

Serves 4 - 6

Tools: knife/ board/ pan

Preparation 10 minutes, cooking 15 minutes, totol 25 minutes

INGREDIENTS:

- 2 onions
- 1 carrot
- 1 stick celery
- 1 red and 1 green pepper
- 250g mushrooms (I prefer to use chestnut mushrooms for flavour and they hold their texture)
- 3 chillies or 3 teaspoons of chilli powder
- 2 tins of cooked beans in water (cannellini, kidney or black), or soak your own the day before and cook thoroughly before using
- 2 tins tomatoes
- 4 teaspoons of vegan low salt bouillon powder
- 3 tablespoons tomato puree
- Optional spices: turmeric/ cumin/ paprika/ cinnamon/ dark (70%) chocolate or 2 tablespoons raw cacao powder

METHOD:

1. Chop 2 onions, 4 cloves of garlic and fry them on a low heat with a tablespoon of oil. As they simmer continue to chop a red and green pepper, 250g mushrooms (or a packet), 3 chillies depending on heat or 3 teaspoons of chilli powder. Stir and fry for a minute.

2. Drain a tin of cannellini beans, a tin of kidney or black beans, 2 tins of tomatoes and add them all to the pan with 1 tin of water and 3 tablespoons tomato puree. Add lots of black pepper, a teaspoon of cumin, a teaspoon of paprika, a teaspoon of turmeric, ½ a teaspoon of cinnamon and 30g of 70% or greater darkest chocolate or 2 tablespoons of raw cacao powder mixed to a paste with water.

3. Add 4 teaspoons vegan bouillon, stir and simmer for 10 minutes.

4. Like many stews and curries this is often better put in the fridge when its cooled and heated up to enjoy the next day.

5. Serve with boiled white or brown basmati rice, guacamole and a few nachos.

6. I also like it with a baked sweet potato.

7. Option to sprinkle with vegan cheese.

GLUTEN FREE

STIR FRY

Tools: Knife/ Board/ wok or large pan/ pan/ grater

Serves 4

Preparation 10 minutes, cooking 15 minutes, total 25 minutes

INGREDIENTS:

- 1 cup brown rice cooked with 2 ½ cups water
- 1 onion
- 2 peppers
- 150g baby corn or a tin of sweetcorn, drained
- 200g mushrooms
- 2 small courgettes or a head of broccoli
- 1 bag of beansprouts
- 200g spinach
- 1 frozen bag of vegan quorn, block of tofu or any meat replacement (optional).
- Garlic, ginger, chilli, coriander, soy sauce (see recipe)

METHOD:

1. Put the rice on. I like brown basmati because it's nutty and good for fibre and it'll be ready by the time you have prepped and cooked the veggies.

2. Chop an onion, a red and green pepper, baby corn, mushrooms, courgette or broccoli and prep your spices.

3. Check your rice.

4. Heat up 2 tablespoons of oil or water in a wok till it's sizzling and add the veggies, quorn or tofu if using and stir continuously. If it starts to stick add a tablespoon of water.

5. Add the spices and continue to stir-fry! There are no rules here but for flavour its best to include: 4 garlic cloves, finely chopped, a 2 inch piece of ginger, peeled with a spoon and grated on the block grater small side or a zester, 2 chillies finely chopped or use frozen ready chopped and a tablespoon of fresh or frozen coriander.

6. Roughly chop the spinach leaves and add them to the wok with a bag of beansprouts.

7. The pan will seem pretty full but don't worry as the veggies will start to collapse. If you have a lid cover the pan now to help the beansprouts cook in steam and you can turn the heat off after a minute.

8. Add a tablespoon of soy sauce and a sprinkle of sesame oil if you wish.

9. Put 3 tablespoons of rice in a bowl, heap your stir-fry onto it and top with crushed nuts and a little fresh coriander or lime.

TAKE-AWAY STYLE 'CHICKN' CURRY

This delicious curry is simple and with only a few ingredients, it's quick, tasty and makes a great transitional recipe, saving money whilst losing none of the tastes-like takeaway flavour.

Serves 4

Tools: Knife, Board, Frying pan or wok

Preparation 5 minutes, cooking 10 minutes, total 15 minutes

INGREDIENTS:

- 1 large onion
- 200g mushrooms
- 2 green peppers
- Either one packet of vegan quorn, Iceland's own brand Chickn fillets or more vegetables (carrots, Chinese cabbage, mange tout, sweet potato)
- Chinese-style curry powder or paste made up to 2 cups
- Optional tin of chopped tomatoes

METHOD:

1. Chop the vegetables and add to a hot pan or wok containing 2 tablespoons water. Add the chicken substitute and cook for 5 minutes. Make up the curry as instructed to 2 cups, add to the pan and stir as it thickens. You may need to add black pepper to taste or a little more water.

2. Serve with boiled rice.

Alternatively, mix with 2 cups of cooked boiled rice and allow to cool. Cook a sheet of puff pastry as per packet instructions (most packet pastries are vegan). When it's cool, remove a thick top layer, fill with curry and cut into 6 pieces. This is a messy but delicious party food.

See 'Cuffy Puff' recipe (Page 15)

AUBERGINE CURRY

If you have time to char the aubergines first this curry takes on a different depth of flavour that I love but it tastes delicious either way! See the charring veggies section (PAGE REF)

Serves 4-6

Tools: knife/ board/ pan

Preparation 10 minutes, cooking 40 minutes, total 50 minutes

INGREDIENTS:

- Coconut oil
- 2 onions
- 6 baby aubergines or 1-2 large ones
- 4 cloves garlic
- 4 teaspoons curry powder
- 2 tins tomatoes
- Tomato puree
- Fresh coriander
- Chapatti/naan/rice to serve

METHOD:

1. Chop 2 onions in 1.5cm chunks and add to a hot pan with a tablespoon of coconut oil, Keep on high heat and stir till the onions start to char/ turn black. (See Page 4 for charring tips)

2. Slice and cube 6 baby aubergines or one to two larger ones. If you char them first the flavour is different but equally delicious.

3. Add this and 4 cloves of chopped garlic to the pan and put a lid on.

4. It will take 5-10 minutes for the aubergine to start to soften then add 4 teaspoons of curry powder.

5. Let that sweat for a minute and then add 2 tins of tomatoes, rinse them out with a cup of water and add that too and a tablespoon of tomato puree.

6. Simmer on a low heat for 20 minutes.

7. You can turn it off at this stage, let it cool and store in the fridge for a few days.

8. Boil brown or white basmati rice and heat one or two naans or 4 chapattis in the oven to make ample accompaniments to serve with the curry.

9. Chop fresh coriander and stir into the warm curry just before you serve it.

VEGETABLE CURRY

A great recipe to use whatever vegetables you like.

Serves 4 hungry people

Tools: knife/ board/ pan

Preparation 5 minutes, cooking 30 minutes, total 35 minutes

INGREDIENTS:

- 2 large onions
- Coconut oil
- 1 red pepper
- 1 green pepper
- 500g okra (frozen or fresh)
- A packet (200g) of chestnut mushrooms
- 4 teaspoons of curry powder
- 1 tablespoon tomato puree
- 1 tin chopped tomatoes
- 2 teaspoons vegetable bouillon
- Salt and Pepper
- Fresh coriander (optional)

METHOD:

1. Chop 2 onions in 1.5cm chunks and add to a hot pan with a tablespoon of coconut oil, Keep on high heat and stir till the onions start to char/ turn black.

2. Chop any veg you like! I would choose a red and green pepper, 500g of okra and a packet of chestnut mushrooms.

3. Chop and add these to the pan with 4 teaspoons of curry powder. I use Mattas international supermarket on Bold Street pre made mix.

4. Stir and sweat with the lid on for a minute.

5. Add a tin of chopped tomatoes, a tin of water, 2 teaspoons of vegan bouillon, a tablespoon of tomato puree and bring to the boil.

6. Simmer for 20 minutes.

7. Boil some brown basmati rice and heat a naan bread or some chapattis in the oven.

8. Chop fresh coriander and stir into the curry just before you serve it.

CAULIFLOWER CURRY

Tools: knife/ board/ pan

Preparation 5 minutes , cooking 20 minutes, total 25 minutes

INGREDIENTS:

- 2 large onions
- 1 tablespoon coconut oil (optional)
- 4 teaspoons curry powder
- A whole cauliflower
- 1 tin of chopped tomatoes
- 1 tablespoon tomato puree
- 2 teaspoons vegetable bouillion
- 2 tablespoons fresh coriander
- Salt and Pepper

METHOD:

1. Chop 2 onions in 1.5cm chunks and add to a hot pan with a tablespoon of coconut oil or omit the oil. Keep on a high heat and stir until the onions start to char/ turn black. Add 4 teaspoons curry powder and cook with lid on for a minute.

2. Chop a cauliflower into 4x4cm pieces including the stalk and leaves and add to the pan with a tin of tomatoes, a tin of water, a tablespoon of tomato puree, 2 teaspoons veggie stock (vegan bouillon), optional- an extra fresh chilli and cook for 15 minutes. Chop a handful of coriander finely and add at the end.

3. A variation on this is to add 2 teaspoons more curry powder at the beginning, omit the water then add a bag of spinach, a tin of drained chick peas and a tin of coconut milk 2 minutes before the end.

4. If it seems too runny reduce the water next time.

TOO-EASY THAI CURRY

Serves 4

Tools: knife/ board/ large deep frying pan or wok/ grater

Preparation 10 minutes, cooking 10 minutes, total 20 minutes

INGREDIENTS:

- 2-4 tablespoons Thai curry paste depending on your particular paste, check the instructions.
- 1 tablespoon coconut oil or water
- 7-10 spring onions, depends on size, I have had giant ones and only needed 2, but you want 2 cupfuls
- 200g mushrooms
- 2 peppers, green, red or yellow
- 200g baby corn or a tin of sweetcorn
- 200g mange touts or peas
- 200g broccoli florets
- Fresh ginger about 3cm in length/ 1 inch
- 2-4 garlic cloves
- 1 red or green chilli or a couple of bird's eye chillies depending on your preferred heat.
- 1 tin coconut milk.
- 2 teaspoons vegan bouillon powder.
- 200g spinach
- 2 tablespoons fresh or frozen coriander.
- 2 sheets rice noodles or 4 smaller bundles or 2 cups brown basmati rice (enough for 4 portions)
- Chopped cashew or pea-nuts.
- Optional: Thai basil, curry leaves, fresh galangal, ginger,
- The authentic Thai spices and vegetables are not essential but if they are available they add another dimension and freshness to the curry. If using them, add the galangal with the garlic and ginger, add 20 curry leaves to infuse flavour into the coconut milk and add Thai basil at the end with the spinach.

METHOD:

1. Place 2 tablespoons of Thai curry paste in a wok with a tablespoon of coconut oil or water and heat without burning. Peel and chop an inch of ginger, 2 garlic cloves and 2 bird's eye chillies all very finely and add to the pan. When they are sizzling add a tin of coconut milk half a tin of water, 2 teaspoons of vegan bouillon and bring to a gentle boil.

2. Chop the spring onions, mushrooms, peppers, baby corn (into rounds), mange tout (snapped in half) and broccoli florets from a whole head of broccoli.

3. Add half the spring onions and the rest of the chopped veggies and cook for 5-7 minutes. Add the Thai basil, rest of the spring onions, put the lid on and turn the heat off.

4. Boil a pan of water for some rice noodles or cook some brown or white basmati rice.

5. Taste the curry, the chunks of spices can be removed or left in at this stage. Chop and stir in the raw spinach and a handful of chopped coriander.

6. To serve, fill a bowl with a portion of rice or noodles, a couple of ladles of curry and top with some chopped raw cashews or peanuts that have toasted in a pan for a few minutes and a wedge of lime.

This recipe is versatile and quick; changing the vegetables and increasing the spice to suit you is easy.

It works really well with chopped butternut squash, but part cook it by boiling for 10 minutes first. If you miss the meaty chew add chopped tempeh, quorn pieces or flavoured tofu by marinating cubes in soy, chilli flakes and nutritional yeast before baking in a hot oven for 10 minutes and adding at the end.

BLIND BEEF STEW

The jackfruit is optional but will certainly give a meatier, stringy texture to the dish and could confuse any meat eater into believing it's beef. It is delicious.

Serves 4.

Tools: knife/board/ large pot for the stove with lid or the oven.

Preparation 10 minutes, cooking 20 minutes, total 30minutes

INGREDIENTS:

- 2-3 Peppers
- 1 large onion
- 4 celery sticks
- 4 large carrots
- 2 tins of jackfruit, drained and grated
- 2-4 cloves of garlic
- 4 teaspoons of vegan bouillon
- 2 tablespoons of soy sauce
- 2 tablespoons vegan 'Worcestershire' or henderson's sauce
- 2 tablespoons of tomato puree
- 1 tablespoon of marmite
- 500g Portobello mushrooms or any other type of firm mushroom
- Handful chopped parsley

METHOD:

1. Chop 2-3 peppers, an onion, 4 celery sticks, 4 large carrots and add to a pan with a small amount of water.

2. Keep the heat high. Finely slice 2 cloves of garlic and add this.

3. In a measuring jug add the bouillon, marmite, tomato puree, Henderson's sauce and soy to make a rich, dark gravy. Make up to 500mls and add to the veg. Cook for 10 minutes.

4. Add the grated jackfruit at this stage if you are using it.

5. Slice a 500g packet of portobello mushrooms or whatever type you are using and add them for the last 5 minutes of cooking time when the carrots are softening. Add salt and pepper to taste and top with a handful of chopped parsley.

6. If the sauce needs to thicken options are reduce it by allowing it to boil, stir a few teaspoons of cornflour mixed with cold water in or add some onion gravy granules as a tasty cheat.

Best served with mash and something green that's steamed!

7. Example: Boil a mix of sweet and white potatoes, skin on, in water for 15 minutes then drain, add salt and pepper, a tablespoon of sunflower spread and mash. Taste for seasoning.

8. Chop up a broccoli 'head' stalks and florets and steam over the pan of boiling potatoes for 5- 7 minutes so it is still vibrant green and a bit of a crunch.

SHEPHERD'S PIE BAKED POTATOES

Serves 4

A fun way to serve a classic, but if you are in a rush, just mash the potatoes and pop on top of the mince in a pie dish and brown under the grill.

Tools: Pan with lid/ knife/ board/ baking tray. Oven at 190 degrees C

Preparation 15 minutes, cooking 1 hr 15mins, total 1hr 30 minutes

INGREDIENTS:

- 4 Baking potatoes
- 1 pack mince: lots of options here: dried soya mince/ vegan quorn mince/ supermarket own brand vegan mince but should be around 300g or use 2 tins of drained lentils
- 1 onion
- 2 sticks celery
- 2 carrots
- 2 tablespoons tomato puree
- A tablespoon yeast extract
- 2 teaspoons vegan bouillon
- Salt and black pepper
- Vegan 'worcestershire' sauce

METHOD:

1. Wash and dry 4 baking potatoes and put them in a hot oven, around 180-200 degrees, for an hour.

2. Remove from the oven and allow to cool before cutting in half lengthwise.

3. Scoop out the soft potato leaving a baked potato boat with about a cm of potato thickness left in the shell.

4. Meanwhile fry a bag of vegan quorn mince or rehydrated soya mince in a tablespoon of oil or water. Keep stirring and remove when 'browned'.

5. Chop an onion, 2 sticks of celery and 2 carrots into small pieces, and add this to the mince or drained lentils along with 2 tablespoons of tomato puree, a tablespoon of marmite or other yeast extract, 2 teaspoons of vegan bouillon, lots black pepper and a glass of water.

6. Simmer for about 10-15 minutes making sure it doesn't stick but the carrots soften and the celery almost becomes translucent.

7. Taste for flavour and add a tablespoon or two of vegan 'worcestershire' sauce.

8. Spoon this meatless mincey yumminess into the baked potato cases. You might have to line them up in a deep baking tray to ensure they don't topple.

9. Mash the potato you removed earlier with a spoon of sunflower spread and 2 tablespoons of plant-based milk of your choice.

10. Add salt and pepper to taste and either spoon on top of the filled potatoes in a rustic manner or fill a freezer bag with the mash, snip a tiny corner off and pipe neatly over the tops.

11. Place the potatoes back in the oven to warm through for 10 minutes and crisp the tops. Best served with lots of greens. I would chop up a head of broccoli, maybe a cauliflower and lots of peas. You can make added gravy using instant granules.

EASY COMBO MEALS FOR ONE

Tools: knife/ board/ pan

Preparation 5 minutes, cooking 5-10 minutes total 15 minutes

INGREDIENTS:

Pick One of:

- 1 cup cooked brown basmati rice
- 2 cups cooked pasta
- A large sweet or white potato
- 1 large wholemeal wrap
- 1 cup of cooked quinoa

Add one of these:

- 1 cup tofu
- 1 cup tempeh
- 1 cup tinned or soaked and cooked beans (eg. black, kidney, chick peas)
- 1 cup lentils

To:

- 4 cups green veg (courgette, cabbage, kale, spinach, broccoli, chard)
- 2 cups other veg (peppers, carrots, onion, mushrooms, sweetcorn, beetroot)

And one, some or all:

- Grated 4 cloves garlic,
- 2 inches ginger,
- 2 chillies,
- 4 tomatoes,
- 2 tablespoons soy sauce,
- 2 tablespoons nutritional yeast,
- 1 tablespoon miso paste,
- 2 tablespoons Thai curry paste,
- 1 tablespoon any nuts or seeds.

METHOD:

1. Heat 4 tablespoons of water in a large pan. Add your selection of ingredients chosen from the above lists and heat through, while stirring, for 5 minutes.

2. Eat like this or add a broth of 2 teaspoons of bouillon with 1 cup water or a small tin coconut milk which will go well with the Thai flavours.

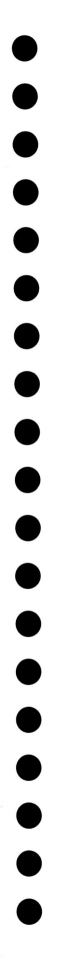

DESSERTS

DIRTY CHOCOLATE BROWNIES

Part of the 'dirty vegan' range, this will make 18 portions.

Tools: Large bowl, hand whisk (balloon style), measuring cups/spoons, sieve, baking tins.

Oven at 170 degrees C.

Prep 10 cooking 25 totoal 35 minutes

INGREDIENTS:

- 2 cups flour
- 2 cups cacao powder
- 1 teaspoon baking powder
- 1 cup brown sugar
- 1 cup caster sugar
- 1 teaspoon salt
- 1 cup sunflower oil and a bit extra to grease tins
- 3 tablespoons vanilla essence or paste
- 1 cup plant milk (cashew/soy/ coconut/ oat)
- 1 cup of the fluid from round a tin of chick peas (aquafaba)
- 1 cup maple syrup
- 2 teaspoons of coffee granules mixed with a tablespoon hot water to dissolve
- Optional add a packet of oreo biscuits, crushed

METHOD:

1. Put the oven on and make sure there are 2 levels you can use.

2. Grease 2 baking tins with sunflower oil.

3. I use an 8" round cake tin with removable bottom and an 8" square one also with a removable bottom because that's what I have and so I don't have to faff with baking paper but if I use a normal tin I do line it as it makes removing them easier.

4. Then.... Sieve all the dry ingredients into a large mixing bowl.

5. Prepare all the wet ingredients in a jug and add to the dry.

6. I use a hand balloon whisk to beat together quickly, don't overbeat. Taste the batter.

7. Sometimes I hold back on the sugar and add more at this stage if needed.

8. Pour into the prepared tins to equal depths-ish.

9. Option to top with chopped chocolate, chocolate chips, nuts, cacao nibs, coconut or anything else you fancy.

10. Pop in oven for 25 mins.

11. Allow to cool in the tin then remove onto a cooling rack.

12. They should be very brownie-like, gooey and delicious if you taste any bits that fall off at this stage!

13. Cut into squares when cool, dust with icing sugar and share.

FRUIT SALAD

Tools: Knife, board, bowl

INGREDIENTS:

Anything you like! Think rainbow.

- Strawberries when in season, raspberries, kiwi, watermelon, mango, pineapple, apples, grapes, oranges, blueberries and tinned fruits in their own juice can also work.

METHOD:

1. Chop it all into bite sized pieces, add a tablespoon of fresh lemon and fresh lime juice and a handful of chopped fresh mint if you fancy.

2. Serve with ice cream, chocolate sauce, coconut cream, cashew cream or dairy-free yogurt.

CHOCOLATE MOUSSE

Tools: Board/ Knife/Blender

Serves 4

INGREDIENTS:

- 4 avocados
- 4 tablespoons cacao
- 8 dates
- 1 tin coconut cream

METHOD:

1. Half 4 avocados and remove the stones.

2. Add 4 tablespoons cacao, 8 dates and a tin of coconut cream and blend till smooooooooooth.

3. Spoon into small cups and put in the fridge for an hour.

4. Too delicious.

CHOCOLATE CHEESECAKE

Serves 8, looks amazing, tastes gorgeous.

Tools: Blender and or food processor, cake tin (preferably one with spring-form base), spatula

INGREDIENTS:

For the base:

- 200g pitted dates
- 200g pecan nuts
- 1 ½ tablespoons cacao
- ½ teaspoon salt
- 2 tablespoons coconut oil

For the topping:

- 4 avocados
- 4 tablespoons cacao powder
- 2- 3 tablespoons date syrup
- 4 tablespoons vegan cream cheese
- 200g fresh raspberries
- Optional- the coconut cream from the top of a tin of coconut- cool the tin in the fridge first then scoop the firm cream off.

METHOD:

1. Line the cake tin with foil or grease with a small amount of vegan butter or oil.

2. Blend the base ingredients making sure you scrape the sides in with the spatula at regular intervals until you have a sticky, crumb like mixture.

3. Press this into the prepared tin and pop in the fridge.

4. Wipe the blender and blade clean and combine the topping ingredients apart from the raspberries. Taste to see if it needs more date syrup. Pour over the base and pop back in the fridge for a good 2-3 hours, ideally 4-6.

5. When ready to serve lift it out of the spring-form tin onto a plate, the layers should show clearly. Top with fresh raspberries, a dusting of cacao and icing sugar, or both. Cut with a warm clean knife (run it under hot water) to keep the layers defined as you serve it.

6. Serve with warm raspberry compote (see below) and cashew or coconut cream.

ROCKY ROAD

This is an absolute favourite and this recipe makes a tray of treats for around 8 people

INGREDIENTS:

- 70g plant based butter- I use vitalite
- 200g dark chocolate- I use 70% but you can get milkier ones without milk solids in.
- 3 tablespoons syrup (golden, rice or date)
- 120g Rich tea biscuits - you will need extra for snacking while chopping.
- 2 bags 'vegan' mini-marshmallows or larger ones you can chop (about 100g)

Optional:

- 120g nuts. I prefer a mix of cashew and brazils (unsalted)
- 40g chopped unsulphured apricots.
- 4 tablespoons icing sugar

You can add any dried fruits to this if you prefer or change to hobnob biscuits or any other combination you come up with. It's hard to beat!

METHOD:

1. Place the chopped chocolate, syrup and butter in a heatproof bowl and sit it over a pan of boiling water so it gets the steam from underneath but isn't touching the water. Apparently you can microwave chocolate but I haven't tried.

2. Stir until its melted and turn off the heat. Take the bowl off the pan.

3. Chop the biscuits, nuts, dried fruit and marshmallows if you haven't sourced mini ones and add them to the chocolate mix. Stir well until everything is smothered in chocolate mix.

4. Line the tray with butter or cling film and press the mixture into it.

5. Pop in the fridge for 3 hours, turn out onto a board covered with icing sugar. Add more icing sugar to the top and spread over before slicing into squares. It is quite rich so think truffle size rather than biscuit or tray bake slab. Roll them in icing sugar and refrigerate what you don't eat immediately.

EASY ICE-CREAM

Tools: Freezer, blender or juicer (or potato masher at a push)

INGREDIENTS:

- 8 over ripe bananas

Optional Flavours:

- 4 Tablespoons cacao powder, or
- 4 tablespoons peanut butter and 100g chocolate chips, or
- Flesh from one mango or 100g of frozen cubes, or
- 100g raspberries

METHOD:

1. Peel and freeze the bananas.

2. I tend to build up a bag of over-ripe bananas over a month as they hit a dark black stage in the fruit bowl. These are perfect for ice-cream as their natural sugars are at a peak!

3. Once frozen the next bit depends on the tools available. You can blend them to a smooth consistency in a blender but I've found if I put it through my juicer (a slow Auger type) it makes a really smooth consistency too. This is perfect to eat right now. If you are going to re-freeze I would add some date syrup.

4. Any of the flavours can be added to make chocolate, peanut butter and chocolate chip, mango or whatever you choose flavours. Just a note that I don't like banana flavoured anything but this is gorgeous and definitely worth a try.

ALTERNATIVE EASY ICE-CREAM

If you can't bear the thought of bananas, this works well and serves one.

Tools: Blender

INGREDIENTS:

- 1 tin coconut milk or cream
- 6 juicy dates (I prefer medjool)

METHOD:

1. Keep the tins of coconut milk or cream in the fridge.

2. Remove the firm top off the coconut milk or spoon out the coconut cream and blend with the dates.

3. Freeze for an hour and enjoy.

CRUMBLE

Makes 4 generous portions

Tools: Bowl/ pie dish/ knife/ Board/ Pan

Preperation 10 minutes, cooking 25 minutes, total 35 minutes

INGREDIENTS:

- 1 cup self –raising flour
- 1 cup almond flour
- 1 cup oats
- 1 cup brown sugar
- 2 teaspoons mixed spice
- 1 – 1 ½ cups vegan butter/ plant-based spread
- Optional flaked almonds

METHOD:

1. Put all the dry ingredients into a bowl, rub the fat into the floury mix so it becomes like breadcrumbs, or like scone mix before you add the milk.

2. Place on top of your fruit, add flaked almonds and bake in the oven at 180 degrees Celsius for around 25 minutes until there's a nice brown crusted top.

3. Serve warm with custard or cream.

APPLE OR RHUBARB CRUMBLE

Tools: knife/ board/ pan

INGREDIENTS:

- 1 kg cooking apples or rhubarb
- When these are seasonal in the UK, plenty of people have a glut of fruit if you ask around.
- 250g sugar (I like using dark brown sugar)
- 3 teaspoons mixed spice

METHOD:

1. To prepare cooking apples, peel the apples and remove the core (pips).

2. Slice them into equal chunks, add the sugar and mixed spice and cook on a low heat until they start to soften. They will cook further in the crumble so it depends how mushy you like your apple as to your starting point. Taste to check on the sweetness.

3. To prepare rhubarb, trim any brown soft bits off and chop into 2cm chunks. Add to a pan with the sugar and mixed spice and heat gently until it begins to soften. I like rhubarb really mushy so I will cook this down.

4. Both can be cooled and kept in the fridge to make a crumble anytime or to have with coconut yogurt.

5. For crumble cover the base of a pie dish with the apples or rhubarb to a 2cm depth and top with the crumble mix and bake as above

CUSTARD

Serves 4

Tools: Pan/ whisk

INGREDIENTS:

- 1 pint plant milk, I like 'Oatly barista' as it's creamy
- 1 tablespoon vanilla paste
- 1 tablespoon cornflour
- ½ teaspoon turmeric
- 1 tablespoon sugar

METHOD:

1. Add all the ingredients to a pan, heat gently and whisk until it thickens. Taste.

2. Date syrup is a nice addition to this.

RASPBERRY COMPOTE

Serves 2

Tools: Pan, spoonTools: Pan/ whisk

INGREDIENTS:

- 200g Fresh or frozen raspberries
- 3 tablespoons icing sugar
- 1 teaspoon fresh lemon juice

METHOD:

1. Place the raspberries and lemon juice in a pan and warm through on a low heat for 2 minutes.

2. Add the icing sugar and continue cooking for 5 minutes.

3. For a smoother compote sieve into a bowl and serve warm or allow to cool.

CHOCOLATE SAUCE

This recipe is so simple but once it's cooled in the fridge it's very tempting to dig in with a spoon or a medjool date!

Tools: Pan, measuring cup.

INGREDIENTS:

- 2/3 cup cacao powder
- 3/4 cup caster sugar
- ½ cup water.

METHOD:

1. Sieve the cacao and sugar into a saucepan.
2. Add the water and simmer for 5 minutes stirring all the time. You will feel the sauce thicken. Put it in clean jam jars or containers and store in the fridge.
3. Lovely over anything.

CASHEW CREAM

Tools: blender- can't think of a replacement!

INGREDIENTS:

- 1 cup cashews, soaked in water overnight
- 1 cup water

METHOD:

1. Drain the nuts, blend the nuts with fresh water, put in a bowl and cool in the fridge.

COCONUT CREAM

INGREDIENTS:

- Tin of coconut milk

METHOD:

1. Place a tin of coconut milk in the fridge.
2. Spoon the cream off the top.
3. You can whip this up for a lighter texture.

Appendix